# VISIT OUR WEBSITE

Learn more about our mission and find our latest updates, hot new releases, freebies, and more.
www.thebubble.press

DON'T FORGET TO RATE THE PRODUCT AND LEAVE A COMMENT.

We care about your opinion!
Help us improve our products.

## The Bubble Press
All of our products are crafted
with obsessive attention to detail.

Copyright © 2020

All rights reserved. This book or any portion thereof may not be reproduced or used in any manner whatsoever without the express written permission of the publisher except for the use of brief quotations in a book review.

# Conversion Chart

## Liquid, Volume, Herbs and Spices

| Avoirdupois | Metric | Imperial |
|---|---|---|
| ¼ tsp | | 1.2 ml |
| ½ tsp | | 2.5 ml |
| 1 tsp | | 5.0 ml |
| 1/2 Tbsp (1½ tsp) | | 7.5 ml |
| 1 Tbsp (3 tsp) | 1/2 fl oz | 15 ml |
| 1/8 cup | 1 fl oz | 30 ml |
| 1/4 cup (4 Tbsp) | 2 fl oz | 60 ml |
| 1/3 cup (5 Tbsp) | 2½ fl oz | 80 ml |
| 1/2 cup (8 Tbsp) | 4 fl oz | 120 ml |
| 2/3 cup (10 Tbsp) | 5 fl oz | 160 ml |
| 3/4 cup (12 Tbsp) | 6 fl oz | 180 ml |
| 1 cup (16 Tbsp) | 8 fl oz (½ a pint) | 250 ml |
| 1¼ cups | 10 fl oz | 300 ml |
| 1½ cups | 12 fl oz | 350 ml |
| 2 cups | 16 fl oz (1 pint) | 475 ml |
| 2½ cups | 20 fl oz | 625 ml |
| 3 cups | 24 fl oz (1½ a pints) | 700 ml |
| 4 cups | 32 fl oz (1 quart) | 950 ml |
| 4 quarts | 128 fl oz (1 gallon) | 3.8 l |

## Weight

| Avoirdupois | Metric |
|---|---|
| ¼ oz | 7 g |
| ½ oz | 15 g |
| 1 oz | 30 g |
| 2 oz | 55 g |
| 3 oz | 85 g |
| 4 ozs (¼ lb) | 115 g |
| 5 ozs (⅓ lb) | 140 g |
| 6 oz | 170 g |
| 7 oz | 200 g |
| 8 ozs (½ lb) | 225 g |
| 9 oz | 255 g |
| 10 ozs (⅔ lb) | 300 g |
| 11 oz | 310 g |
| 12 ozs (¾ lb) | 340 g |
| 13 oz | 370 g |
| 14 oz | 400 g |
| 15 oz | 425 g |
| 16 ozs (1 lb) | 450 g |
| 2 pounds | 900 g |

## Temperature

| °F | °C |
|---|---|
| 200 | 90 |
| 250 | 120 |
| 300 | 150 |
| 325 | 175 |
| 350 | 180 |
| 375 | 190 |
| 400 | 200 |
| 435 | 220 |
| 450 | 230 |
| 475 | 250 |
| 500 | 260 |

## Baking Pan Size

| Shape | US | Volume | Metric | Volume |
|---|---|---|---|---|
| Round | 8 x 2 inches | 6 cups | 20 x 5 cm | 1.4 liters |
| Round | 9 x 2 inches | 8 cups | 23 x 5 cm | 1.9 liters |
| Round | 10 x 2 inches | 1 cup | 25 x 5 cm | 2.6 liters |
| Square | 8 x 8 x 2 inches | 8 cups | 20 x 20 x 5 cm | 1.9 liters |
| Square | 9 x 9 x 2 inches | 10 cups | 23 x 23 x 5 cm | 2.4 liters |
| Square | 10 x 10 x 2 inches | 12 cups | 25 x 25 x 5 cm | 2.8 liters |
| Rectangular | 11 x 7 x 2 inches | 6 cups | 28 x 18 x 5 cm | 1.4 liters |
| Rectangular | 13 x 9 x 2 inches | 4 cups | 33 x 23 x 5 cm | 3.3 liters |

**Please Note:** Conversions are not exact, they are rounded slightly for ease.

# Table of Contents

|  | | Main course | Baking | Starter | Dessert |
|---|---|:---:|:---:|:---:|:---:|
| Recipe | | | | | |
| 01 | Page 10 | ☐ | ☐ | ☐ | ☐ |
|  |  | ☆ ☆ ☆ ☆ ☆ | | | |
| 02 | Page 12 | ☐ | ☐ | ☐ | ☐ |
|  |  | ☆ ☆ ☆ ☆ ☆ | | | |
| 03 | Page 14 | ☐ | ☐ | ☐ | ☐ |
|  |  | ☆ ☆ ☆ ☆ ☆ | | | |
| 04 | Page 16 | ☐ | ☐ | ☐ | ☐ |
|  |  | ☆ ☆ ☆ ☆ ☆ | | | |
| 05 | Page 18 | ☐ | ☐ | ☐ | ☐ |
|  |  | ☆ ☆ ☆ ☆ ☆ | | | |
| 06 | Page 20 | ☐ | ☐ | ☐ | ☐ |
|  |  | ☆ ☆ ☆ ☆ ☆ | | | |
| 07 | Page 22 | ☐ | ☐ | ☐ | ☐ |
|  |  | ☆ ☆ ☆ ☆ ☆ | | | |
| 08 | Page 24 | ☐ | ☐ | ☐ | ☐ |
|  |  | ☆ ☆ ☆ ☆ ☆ | | | |

## Table of Contents

| Recipe | | Main course | Baking | Starter | Dessert |
|---|---|---|---|---|---|
| 09 | Page 26 | ☐ ☆☆☆☆☆ | ☐ | ☐ | ☐ |
| 10 | Page 28 | ☐ ☆☆☆☆☆ | ☐ | ☐ | ☐ |
| 11 | Page 30 | ☐ ☆☆☆☆☆ | ☐ | ☐ | ☐ |
| 12 | Page 32 | ☐ ☆☆☆☆☆ | ☐ | ☐ | ☐ |
| 13 | Page 34 | ☐ ☆☆☆☆☆ | ☐ | ☐ | ☐ |
| 14 | Page 36 | ☐ ☆☆☆☆☆ | ☐ | ☐ | ☐ |
| 15 | Page 38 | ☐ ☆☆☆☆☆ | ☐ | ☐ | ☐ |
| 16 | Page 40 | ☐ ☆☆☆☆☆ | ☐ | ☐ | ☐ |

## Table of Contents

| Recipe | | Main course | Baking | Starter | Dessert |
|---|---|---|---|---|---|
| 17 | Page 42 | ☐ | ☐ | ☐ | ☐ |
| | | ☆☆☆☆☆ | | | |
| 18 | Page 44 | ☐ | ☐ | ☐ | ☐ |
| | | ☆☆☆☆☆ | | | |
| 19 | Page 46 | ☐ | ☐ | ☐ | ☐ |
| | | ☆☆☆☆☆ | | | |
| 20 | Page 48 | ☐ | ☐ | ☐ | ☐ |
| | | ☆☆☆☆☆ | | | |
| 21 | Page 50 | ☐ | ☐ | ☐ | ☐ |
| | | ☆☆☆☆☆ | | | |
| 22 | Page 52 | ☐ | ☐ | ☐ | ☐ |
| | | ☆☆☆☆☆ | | | |
| 23 | Page 54 | ☐ | ☐ | ☐ | ☐ |
| | | ☆☆☆☆☆ | | | |
| 24 | Page 56 | ☐ | ☐ | ☐ | ☐ |
| | | ☆☆☆☆☆ | | | |

## Table of Contents

|  |  | Main course | Baking | Starter | Dessert |
|---|---|---|---|---|---|
| Recipe |  |  |  |  |  |
| 25 | Page 58 | ☐ ☐ ☐ ☐ ☆☆☆☆☆ | | | |
| 26 | Page 60 | ☐ ☐ ☐ ☐ ☆☆☆☆☆ | | | |
| 27 | Page 62 | ☐ ☐ ☐ ☐ ☆☆☆☆☆ | | | |
| 28 | Page 64 | ☐ ☐ ☐ ☐ ☆☆☆☆☆ | | | |
| 29 | Page 66 | ☐ ☐ ☐ ☐ ☆☆☆☆☆ | | | |
| 30 | Page 68 | ☐ ☐ ☐ ☐ ☆☆☆☆☆ | | | |
| 31 | Page 70 | ☐ ☐ ☐ ☐ ☆☆☆☆☆ | | | |
| 32 | Page 72 | ☐ ☐ ☐ ☐ ☆☆☆☆☆ | | | |

# Table of Contents

|  | Recipe |  | Main course | Baking | Starter | Dessert |
|---|---|---|---|---|---|---|
| 33 | Page 74 | ☆☆☆☆☆ | ☐ | ☐ | ☐ | ☐ |
| 34 | Page 76 | ☆☆☆☆☆ | ☐ | ☐ | ☐ | ☐ |
| 35 | Page 78 | ☆☆☆☆☆ | ☐ | ☐ | ☐ | ☐ |
| 36 | Page 80 | ☆☆☆☆☆ | ☐ | ☐ | ☐ | ☐ |
| 37 | Page 82 | ☆☆☆☆☆ | ☐ | ☐ | ☐ | ☐ |
| 38 | Page 84 | ☆☆☆☆☆ | ☐ | ☐ | ☐ | ☐ |
| 39 | Page 86 | ☆☆☆☆☆ | ☐ | ☐ | ☐ | ☐ |
| 40 | Page 88 | ☆☆☆☆☆ | ☐ | ☐ | ☐ | ☐ |

# Table of Contents

|  | Recipe |  | Main course | Baking | Starter | Dessert |
|---|---|---|---|---|---|---|
| 41 | Page 90 | | ☐ ☆☆☆☆☆ | ☐ | ☐ | ☐ |
| 42 | Page 92 | | ☐ ☆☆☆☆☆ | ☐ | ☐ | ☐ |
| 43 | Page 94 | | ☐ ☆☆☆☆☆ | ☐ | ☐ | ☐ |
| 44 | Page 96 | | ☐ ☆☆☆☆☆ | ☐ | ☐ | ☐ |
| 45 | Page 98 | | ☐ ☆☆☆☆☆ | ☐ | ☐ | ☐ |
| 46 | Page 100 | | ☐ ☆☆☆☆☆ | ☐ | ☐ | ☐ |
| 47 | Page 102 | | ☐ ☆☆☆☆☆ | ☐ | ☐ | ☐ |
| 48 | Page 104 | | ☐ ☆☆☆☆☆ | ☐ | ☐ | ☐ |

## Table of Contents

| Recipe | | Main course | Baking | Starter | Dessert |
|---|---|---|---|---|---|
| 49 | Page 106 | ☐ ☆☆☆☆☆ | ☐ | ☐ | ☐ |
| 50 | Page 108 | ☐ ☆☆☆☆☆ | ☐ | ☐ | ☐ |
| 51 | Page 110 | ☐ ☆☆☆☆☆ | ☐ | ☐ | ☐ |
| 52 | Page 112 | ☐ ☆☆☆☆☆ | ☐ | ☐ | ☐ |
| 53 | Page 114 | ☐ ☆☆☆☆☆ | ☐ | ☐ | ☐ |
| 54 | Page 116 | ☐ ☆☆☆☆☆ | ☐ | ☐ | ☐ |
| 55 | Page 118 | ☐ ☆☆☆☆☆ | ☐ | ☐ | ☐ |
| 56 | Page 120 | ☐ ☆☆☆☆☆ | ☐ | ☐ | ☐ |

# Table of Contents

| Recipe | | Main course | Baking | Starter | Dessert |
|---|---|---|---|---|---|
| 57 | Page 122 | ☐ ☆☆☆☆☆ | ☐ | ☐ | ☐ |
| 58 | Page 124 | ☐ ☆☆☆☆☆ | ☐ | ☐ | ☐ |
| 59 | Page 126 | ☐ ☆☆☆☆☆ | ☐ | ☐ | ☐ |
| 60 | Page 128 | ☐ ☆☆☆☆☆ | ☐ | ☐ | ☐ |
| 61 | Page 130 | ☐ ☆☆☆☆☆ | ☐ | ☐ | ☐ |
| 62 | Page 132 | ☐ ☆☆☆☆☆ | ☐ | ☐ | ☐ |
| 63 | Page 134 | ☐ ☆☆☆☆☆ | ☐ | ☐ | ☐ |
| 64 | Page 136 | ☐ ☆☆☆☆☆ | ☐ | ☐ | ☐ |

## 01

**Name:** Easy One-Pan Coconut Curry
**Date:** _____  **Source:** _____

- [x] Main Course
- [ ] Baking
- [ ] Starter
- [ ] Dessert

**Servings:** 2   **Prep Time:** _____   **Cook Time:** _____

### Ingredients

1 teaspoon gavan

2 Large Potatoes (Cubed)
1 Can Chickpeas
½ brown Onion (diced)
70g button mushrooms (diced)
500ml Coconut cream
125ml Vegetable Stock
2-3 tablespoon Maple Syrup
1-2 bay leaves

**Difficulty:** ■ ☐ ☐ ☐ ☐

### Notes

You can add more or less Coconut Cream to your desired consistency.
The Curry will reduce once you let it sit

## Directions

1. Fry chickpeas and onion in oil
2. Add Rest of ingrediets  Simmer 10min
3. Add Potatoes and Stir in
4. Remove from heat allow to Cool

Serve on bed of Jasmine Rice

Rating: ★ ★ ★ ★ ☆

Notes

**Name:** LENTIL BOLOGNESE

**Date:** 2     **Source:**

- [x] Main Course
- [ ] Baking
- [ ] Starter
- [ ] Dessert

Servings: ___     Prep Time: ___     Cook Time: ___

## Ingredients

- 1 brown onion, finely diced
- 2 garlic cloves, minced
- 1–2 tablespoons vegan butter
- 70g (1 cup) button mushrooms, finely diced
- 40g (½ cup) aubergine (eggplant), finely diced
- 250ml (1 cup) salt-reduced tomato paste
- 125ml (½ cup) vegetable stock, plus more if needed
- 1 teaspoon dried sage
- 1 teaspoon dried thyme
- ½ teaspoon dried oregano
- 2 teaspoons smoked paprika
- 1 teaspoon ground nutmeg
- ½ teaspoon ground cloves
- 1 tablespoon nutritional yeast
- 1½ tablespoons coconut sugar
- 2 × 400g (14oz) cans brown lentils, rinsed and drained
- salt and pepper, to taste

**Difficulty:** ■ ☐ ☐ ☐ ☐

**Notes:** Can swap Aubergine for Corgette

## Directions

1. Brown the Onion and Garlic, butter Add Mushrooms, aubergine, tomatoe paste, Stock, herbs, spices
2. Simmer on medium heat 3-4 mins
3. Add Coconut Sugar and lentils Simmer 5-6 mins
4. Add little water if becomes too thick or sticks
5. Serve with GF Pasta or Rice

Rating: ★ ★ ★ ★ ☆

Notes

03

Name: ....................................................................................

Date: ........................  Source: ...........................................

☐ Main Course   ☐ Baking   ☐ Starter   ☐ Dessert

Servings: ................   Prep Time: ................   Cook Time: ................

## Ingredients

Difficulty: ☐ ☐ ☐ ☐ ☐

Notes

# Directions

Rating: ☆ ☆ ☆ ☆ ☆

Notes

| 04 | Name: |
|---|---|
| | Date: _____ Source: _____ |

☐ Main Course  ☐ Baking  ☐ Starter  ☐ Dessert

Servings: _____  Prep Time: _____  Cook Time: _____

## Ingredients

_____   _____
_____   _____
_____   _____
_____   _____
_____   _____
_____   _____
_____   _____

Difficulty: ☐ ☐ ☐ ☐ ☐

**Notes**

# Directions

Rating: ☆ ☆ ☆ ☆ ☆

Notes

**05**

Name: _____

Date: _____  Source: _____

☐ Main Course  ☐ Baking  ☐ Starter  ☐ Dessert

Servings: _____  Prep Time: _____  Cook Time: _____

## Ingredients

Difficulty: ☐ ☐ ☐ ☐ ☐

Notes

## Directions

Rating: ☆ ☆ ☆ ☆ ☆

Notes

| 06 | Name: _____ |
|---|---|
| | Date: _____ Source: _____ |

☐ Main Course  ☐ Baking  ☐ Starter  ☐ Dessert

Servings: _____   Prep Time: _____   Cook Time: _____

## Ingredients

_____

_____

_____

_____

_____

_____

_____

_____

Difficulty: ☐ ☐ ☐ ☐ ☐

Notes

# Directions

Rating: ☆ ☆ ☆ ☆ ☆

Notes

| 07 | **Name:** ........................................................................... |
|---|---|
| | **Date:** ....................... **Source:** ............................... |

☐ Main Course  ☐ Baking  ☐ Starter  ☐ Dessert

**Servings:** ...................  **Prep Time:** ...................  **Cook Time:** ...................

## Ingredients

........................................................    ........................................................
........................................................    ........................................................
........................................................    ........................................................
........................................................    ........................................................
........................................................    ........................................................
........................................................    ........................................................
........................................................    ........................................................
........................................................    ........................................................

**Difficulty:** ☐ ☐ ☐ ☐ ☐

**Notes**

## Directions

Rating: ☆ ☆ ☆ ☆ ☆

Notes

| 08 | Name: _____ |
|---|---|
| | Date: _____ Source: _____ |

☐ Main Course   ☐ Baking   ☐ Starter   ☐ Dessert

Servings: _____   Prep Time: _____   Cook Time: _____

## Ingredients

_____   _____

_____   _____

_____   _____

_____   _____

_____   _____

_____   _____

_____   _____

_____   _____

Difficulty: ☐ ☐ ☐ ☐ ☐

Notes

# Directions

Rating: ☆ ☆ ☆ ☆ ☆

Notes

## 09

**Name:** ..........................................................................................

**Date:** ........................  **Source:** ..................................................

☐ Main Course  ☐ Baking  ☐ Starter  ☐ Dessert

**Servings:** ....................  **Prep Time:** ....................  **Cook Time:** ....................

## Ingredients

..........................................................  ..........................................................

..........................................................  ..........................................................

..........................................................  ..........................................................

..........................................................  ..........................................................

..........................................................  ..........................................................

..........................................................  ..........................................................

..........................................................  ..........................................................

**Difficulty:** ☐ ☐ ☐ ☐ ☐

**Notes**

# Directions

Rating: ☆ ☆ ☆ ☆ ☆

Notes

| 10 | Name: |
|---|---|
| | Date: _____ Source: _____ |

☐ Main Course  ☐ Baking  ☐ Starter  ☐ Dessert

Servings: _____  Prep Time: _____  Cook Time: _____

## Ingredients

Difficulty: ☐ ☐ ☐ ☐ ☐

Notes

# Directions

Rating: ☆ ☆ ☆ ☆ ☆

Notes

| 11 | Name: |
|---|---|
| | Date: _____ Source: _____ |

☐ Main Course  ☐ Baking  ☐ Starter  ☐ Dessert

Servings: _____  Prep Time: _____  Cook Time: _____

## Ingredients

Difficulty: ☐ ☐ ☐ ☐ ☐

Notes

# Directions

Rating: ☆ ☆ ☆ ☆ ☆

Notes

| 12 | Name: |
|---|---|
| | Date: _____ Source: _____ |
| | ☐ Main Course  ☐ Baking  ☐ Starter  ☐ Dessert |

Servings: _____    Prep Time: _____    Cook Time: _____

### Ingredients

Difficulty: ☐ ☐ ☐ ☐ ☐

Notes

# Directions

Rating: ☆ ☆ ☆ ☆ ☆

Notes

| 13 | Name: |
|---|---|
| | Date: _____ Source: _____ |

☐ Main Course  ☐ Baking  ☐ Starter  ☐ Dessert

Servings: _____   Prep Time: _____   Cook Time: _____

## Ingredients

Difficulty: ☐ ☐ ☐ ☐ ☐

Notes

## Directions

Rating: ☆ ☆ ☆ ☆ ☆

Notes

**14**

Name: ........................................................................................

Date: ...................... Source: ...............................................

☐ Main Course ☐ Baking ☐ Starter ☐ Dessert

Servings: .................. Prep Time: .................. Cook Time: ..................

## Ingredients

Difficulty: ☐ ☐ ☐ ☐ ☐

Notes

## Directions

Rating: ☆ ☆ ☆ ☆ ☆

Notes

| 15 | Name: |
|---|---|
| | Date: _____ Source: _____ |

☐ Main Course  ☐ Baking  ☐ Starter  ☐ Dessert

Servings: _____  Prep Time: _____  Cook Time: _____

## Ingredients

Difficulty: ☐ ☐ ☐ ☐ ☐

Notes

# Directions

Rating: ☆ ☆ ☆ ☆ ☆

Notes

| 16 | Name: |
|---|---|
| | Date: _____ Source: _____ |

☐ Main Course  ☐ Baking  ☐ Starter  ☐ Dessert

Servings: _____  Prep Time: _____  Cook Time: _____

## Ingredients

Difficulty: ☐ ☐ ☐ ☐ ☐

Notes

## Directions

Rating: ☆ ☆ ☆ ☆ ☆

Notes

| 17 | Name: _____ |
|---|---|
|  | Date: _____ Source: _____ |

☐ Main Course ☐ Baking ☐ Starter ☐ Dessert

Servings: _____ Prep Time: _____ Cook Time: _____

## Ingredients

Difficulty: ☐ ☐ ☐ ☐ ☐

### Notes

## Directions

Rating: ☆ ☆ ☆ ☆ ☆

Notes

# 18

**Name:** ................................................

**Date:** ................  **Source:** ................................

- [ ] Main Course
- [ ] Baking
- [ ] Starter
- [ ] Dessert

**Servings:** ............  **Prep Time:** ............  **Cook Time:** ............

## Ingredients

...................................................................................

...................................................................................

...................................................................................

...................................................................................

...................................................................................

...................................................................................

...................................................................................

...................................................................................

**Difficulty:** ☐ ☐ ☐ ☐ ☐

## Notes

## Directions

Rating: ☆ ☆ ☆ ☆ ☆

Notes

| 19 | Name: _____ |
|---|---|
| | Date: _____ Source: _____ |

☐ Main Course ☐ Baking ☐ Starter ☐ Dessert

Servings: _____ Prep Time: _____ Cook Time: _____

## Ingredients

Difficulty: ☐ ☐ ☐ ☐ ☐

### Notes

## Directions

**Rating:** ☆ ☆ ☆ ☆ ☆

Notes

**20**

Name: ........................................................................

Date: ....................  Source: ........................................

☐ Main Course  ☐ Baking  ☐ Starter  ☐ Dessert

Servings: ................  Prep Time: ................  Cook Time: ................

## Ingredients

Difficulty: ☐ ☐ ☐ ☐ ☐

Notes

48

# Directions

Rating: ☆ ☆ ☆ ☆ ☆

Notes

| 21 | Name: |
|---|---|
| | Date: _____ Source: |

☐ Main Course  ☐ Baking  ☐ Starter  ☐ Dessert

Servings: _____  Prep Time: _____  Cook Time: _____

## Ingredients

Difficulty: ☐ ☐ ☐ ☐ ☐

### Notes

## Directions

Rating: ☆ ☆ ☆ ☆ ☆

Notes

| 22 | Name: |
|---|---|
| | Date: _____ Source: _____ |

☐ Main Course  ☐ Baking  ☐ Starter  ☐ Dessert

Servings: _____  Prep Time: _____  Cook Time: _____

## Ingredients

Difficulty: ☐ ☐ ☐ ☐ ☐

Notes

# Directions

Rating: ☆ ☆ ☆ ☆ ☆

Notes

| 23 | Name: |
|---|---|
| | Date: _____ Source: _____ |

☐ Main Course  ☐ Baking  ☐ Starter  ☐ Dessert

Servings: _____   Prep Time: _____   Cook Time: _____

## Ingredients

Difficulty: ☐ ☐ ☐ ☐ ☐

Notes

## Directions

Rating: ☆ ☆ ☆ ☆ ☆

Notes

| 24

**Name:** ..................................................................

**Date:** ........................  **Source:** ..................................

☐ Main Course   ☐ Baking   ☐ Starter   ☐ Dessert

Servings: ................  Prep Time: ................  Cook Time: ................

## Ingredients

----

Difficulty: ☐ ☐ ☐ ☐ ☐

**Notes**

## Directions

Rating: ☆ ☆ ☆ ☆ ☆

Notes

# 25

Name: ........................................................................

Date: ....................  Source: ..................................

☐ Main Course  ☐ Baking  ☐ Starter  ☐ Dessert

Servings: ................  Prep Time: ................  Cook Time: ................

## Ingredients

...........................................................................................................

...........................................................................................................

...........................................................................................................

...........................................................................................................

...........................................................................................................

...........................................................................................................

...........................................................................................................

...........................................................................................................

Difficulty: ☐ ☐ ☐ ☐ ☐

Notes

# Directions

Rating: ☆ ☆ ☆ ☆ ☆

Notes

# 26

**Name:** _____

**Date:** _____  **Source:** _____

☐ Main Course   ☐ Baking   ☐ Starter   ☐ Dessert

**Servings:** _____   **Prep Time:** _____   **Cook Time:** _____

## Ingredients

_____    _____
_____    _____
_____    _____
_____    _____
_____    _____
_____    _____
_____    _____
_____    _____

**Difficulty:** ☐ ☐ ☐ ☐ ☐

**Notes**

# Directions

Rating: ☆ ☆ ☆ ☆ ☆

Notes

| 27 | Name: _____
| | Date: _____  Source: _____

☐ Main Course  ☐ Baking  ☐ Starter  ☐ Dessert

Servings: _____  Prep Time: _____  Cook Time: _____

## Ingredients

Difficulty: ☐ ☐ ☐ ☐ ☐

Notes

## Directions

Rating: ☆ ☆ ☆ ☆ ☆

Notes

| 28 | Name: _____ |
| Date: _____ Source: _____ |

☐ Main Course   ☐ Baking   ☐ Starter   ☐ Dessert

Servings: _____   Prep Time: _____   Cook Time: _____

## Ingredients

Difficulty: ☐ ☐ ☐ ☐ ☐

### Notes

## Directions

Rating: ☆ ☆ ☆ ☆ ☆

Notes

| 29 | Name: |
|---|---|
| | Date: _____ Source: _____ |
| | ☐ Main Course   ☐ Baking   ☐ Starter   ☐ Dessert |

Servings: _____   Prep Time: _____   Cook Time: _____

## Ingredients

Difficulty: ☐ ☐ ☐ ☐ ☐

**Notes**

# Directions

Rating: ☆ ☆ ☆ ☆ ☆

Notes

Name: .................................................................................

Date: ........................  Source: ...............................................

☐ Main Course   ☐ Baking   ☐ Starter   ☐ Dessert

Servings: ..................   Prep Time: ..................   Cook Time: ..................

## Ingredients

Difficulty: ☐ ☐ ☐ ☐ ☐

Notes

## Directions

Rating: ☆ ☆ ☆ ☆ ☆

Notes

| 31 | Name: |
|---|---|
| | Date: Source: |

☐ Main Course　　☐ Baking　　☐ Starter　　☐ Dessert

Servings: ............　Prep Time: ............　Cook Time: ............

### Ingredients

Difficulty: ☐ ☐ ☐ ☐ ☐

Notes

## Directions

Rating: ☆ ☆ ☆ ☆ ☆

Notes

| 32 | Name: _____ |
|---|---|
| | Date: _____ Source: _____ |

☐ Main Course  ☐ Baking  ☐ Starter  ☐ Dessert

Servings: _____  Prep Time: _____  Cook Time: _____

### Ingredients

_____   _____
_____   _____
_____   _____
_____   _____
_____   _____
_____   _____
_____   _____
_____   _____

Difficulty: ☐ ☐ ☐ ☐ ☐

### Notes

# Directions

Rating: ☆ ☆ ☆ ☆ ☆

Notes

| 33 | Name: |
|---|---|
| | Date:      Source: |

- ☐ Main Course    ☐ Baking    ☐ Starter    ☐ Dessert

Servings:     Prep Time:     Cook Time:

## Ingredients

Difficulty: ☐ ☐ ☐ ☐ ☐

Notes

## Directions

Rating: ☆ ☆ ☆ ☆ ☆

Notes

| 34 | Name: |
|---|---|
| | Date:        Source: |

☐ Main Course    ☐ Baking    ☐ Starter    ☐ Dessert

Servings:        Prep Time:        Cook Time:

## Ingredients

Difficulty: ☐ ☐ ☐ ☐ ☐

**Notes**

## Directions

Rating: ☆ ☆ ☆ ☆ ☆

Notes

**Name:**

**Date:** _____ **Source:** _____

☐ Main Course  ☐ Baking  ☐ Starter  ☐ Dessert

**Servings:** _____ **Prep Time:** _____ **Cook Time:** _____

## Ingredients

**Difficulty:** ☐ ☐ ☐ ☐ ☐

**Notes**

## Directions

Rating: ☆ ☆ ☆ ☆ ☆

Notes

36

Name: ........................................................
Date: ............... Source: ...............................

☐ Main Course  ☐ Baking  ☐ Starter  ☐ Dessert

Servings: ............ Prep Time: ............ Cook Time: ............

### Ingredients

Difficulty: ☐ ☐ ☐ ☐ ☐

Notes

## Directions

Rating: ☆ ☆ ☆ ☆ ☆

Notes

**37**

Name:

Date:　　　　　　　　Source:

☐ Main Course　　☐ Baking　　☐ Starter　　☐ Dessert

Servings:　　　　Prep Time:　　　　Cook Time:

## Ingredients

Difficulty: ☐ ☐ ☐ ☐ ☐

Notes

## Directions

Rating: ☆ ☆ ☆ ☆ ☆

Notes

| 38 | Name: |
|---|---|
| | Date: Source: |

☐ Main Course  ☐ Baking  ☐ Starter  ☐ Dessert

Servings: ____  Prep Time: ____  Cook Time: ____

### Ingredients

Difficulty: ☐ ☐ ☐ ☐ ☐

### Notes

# Directions

Rating: ☆ ☆ ☆ ☆ ☆

Notes

| | Name: | | |
|---|---|---|---|
| **39** | Date: | Source: | |
| | ☐ Main Course ☐ Baking | ☐ Starter ☐ Dessert | |

Servings: _____   Prep Time: _____   Cook Time: _____

## Ingredients

Difficulty: ☐ ☐ ☐ ☐ ☐

### Notes

# Directions

Rating: ☆ ☆ ☆ ☆ ☆

Notes

| | Name: |
|---|---|
| 40 | Date: _____ Source: _____ |

☐ Main Course  ☐ Baking  ☐ Starter  ☐ Dessert

Servings: _____  Prep Time: _____  Cook Time: _____

## Ingredients

Difficulty: ☐ ☐ ☐ ☐ ☐

Notes

## Directions

Rating: ☆ ☆ ☆ ☆ ☆

Notes

# 41

**Name:**

**Date:** **Source:**

- ☐ Main Course
- ☐ Baking
- ☐ Starter
- ☐ Dessert

**Servings:** **Prep Time:** **Cook Time:**

## Ingredients

**Difficulty:** ☐ ☐ ☐ ☐ ☐

### Notes

# Directions

Rating: ☆ ☆ ☆ ☆ ☆

Notes

| 42 | Name: |
|---|---|
| | Date: Source: |
| | ☐ Main Course  ☐ Baking  ☐ Starter  ☐ Dessert |

Servings: _____  Prep Time: _____  Cook Time: _____

## Ingredients

Difficulty: ☐ ☐ ☐ ☐ ☐

Notes

# Directions

Rating: ☆ ☆ ☆ ☆ ☆

Notes

**Name:**

**Date:** _____  **Source:** _____

☐ Main Course  ☐ Baking  ☐ Starter  ☐ Dessert

Servings: _____  Prep Time: _____  Cook Time: _____

## Ingredients

Difficulty: ☐ ☐ ☐ ☐ ☐

### Notes

## Directions

Rating: ☆ ☆ ☆ ☆ ☆

Notes

**Name:**

**Date:** _____  **Source:** _____

☐ Main Course  ☐ Baking  ☐ Starter  ☐ Dessert

**Servings:** _____  **Prep Time:** _____  **Cook Time:** _____

## Ingredients

Difficulty: ☐ ☐ ☐ ☐ ☐

**Notes**

## Directions

Rating: ☆ ☆ ☆ ☆ ☆

Notes

**Name:**

**Date:** _____  **Source:** _____

☐ Main Course  ☐ Baking  ☐ Starter  ☐ Dessert

**Servings:** _____  **Prep Time:** _____  **Cook Time:** _____

## Ingredients

**Difficulty:** ☐ ☐ ☐ ☐ ☐

### Notes

# Directions

Rating: ☆ ☆ ☆ ☆ ☆

Notes

Name:

Date:　　　　　　　Source:

☐ Main Course　　☐ Baking　　☐ Starter　　☐ Dessert

Servings:　　　　Prep Time:　　　　Cook Time:

## Ingredients

Difficulty: ☐ ☐ ☐ ☐ ☐

Notes

# Directions

Rating: ☆ ☆ ☆ ☆ ☆

Notes

**Name:**

**Date:** **Source:**

☐ Main Course ☐ Baking ☐ Starter ☐ Dessert

**Servings:** **Prep Time:** **Cook Time:**

**Ingredients**

Difficulty: ☐ ☐ ☐ ☐ ☐

Notes

# Directions

Rating: ☆ ☆ ☆ ☆ ☆

Notes

| | 48 | Name: |
|---|---|---|
| | | Date:        Source: |

☐ Main Course    ☐ Baking    ☐ Starter    ☐ Dessert

Servings:      Prep Time:      Cook Time:

## Ingredients

Difficulty: ☐ ☐ ☐ ☐ ☐

Notes

## Directions

Rating: ☆ ☆ ☆ ☆ ☆

Notes

| 49 | Name: _____ |
|----|-----------------------------------|
|    | Date: _____ Source: _____ |

- ☐ Main Course   ☐ Baking   ☐ Starter   ☐ Dessert

Servings: _____  Prep Time: _____  Cook Time: _____

## Ingredients

_____   _____
_____   _____
_____   _____
_____   _____
_____   _____
_____   _____
_____   _____

Difficulty: ☐ ☐ ☐ ☐ ☐

Notes

# Directions

Rating: ☆ ☆ ☆ ☆ ☆

Notes

| Name: |
|---|
| Date: | Source: |

- ☐ Main Course
- ☐ Baking
- ☐ Starter
- ☐ Dessert

Servings: _____  Prep Time: _____  Cook Time: _____

## Ingredients

Difficulty: ☐ ☐ ☐ ☐ ☐

Notes

## Directions

Rating: ☆ ☆ ☆ ☆ ☆

Notes

**Name:**

**Date:** _____  **Source:** _____

☐ Main Course  ☐ Baking  ☐ Starter  ☐ Dessert

**Servings:** _____  **Prep Time:** _____  **Cook Time:** _____

### 🧂 Ingredients

**Difficulty:** ☐ ☐ ☐ ☐ ☐

**Notes**

## Directions

Rating: ☆ ☆ ☆ ☆ ☆

Notes

| 52 | Name: |
|---|---|
| | Date: _____  Source: _____ |

☐ Main Course  ☐ Baking  ☐ Starter  ☐ Dessert

Servings: _____  Prep Time: _____  Cook Time: _____

## Ingredients

Difficulty: ☐ ☐ ☐ ☐ ☐

### Notes

# Directions

Rating: ☆ ☆ ☆ ☆ ☆

Notes

Name:

Date: Source:

- ☐ Main Course
- ☐ Baking
- ☐ Starter
- ☐ Dessert

Servings: Prep Time: Cook Time:

## Ingredients

Difficulty: ☐ ☐ ☐ ☐ ☐

Notes

# Directions

Rating: ☆ ☆ ☆ ☆ ☆

Notes

**Name:**

**Date:** _____ **Source:** _____

☐ Main Course  ☐ Baking  ☐ Starter  ☐ Dessert

**Servings:** _____ **Prep Time:** _____ **Cook Time:** _____

**Ingredients**

**Difficulty:** ☐ ☐ ☐ ☐ ☐

**Notes**

# Directions

Rating: ☆ ☆ ☆ ☆ ☆

Notes

| 55 | Name: |
|---|---|
| | Date: _____ Source: _____ |
| | ☐ Main Course   ☐ Baking   ☐ Starter   ☐ Dessert |

Servings: _____   Prep Time: _____   Cook Time: _____

## Ingredients

Difficulty: ☐ ☐ ☐ ☐ ☐

Notes

# Directions

Rating: ☆ ☆ ☆ ☆ ☆

Notes

**Name:**

**Date:** _____ **Source:** _____

☐ Main Course  ☐ Baking  ☐ Starter  ☐ Dessert

**Servings:** _____ **Prep Time:** _____ **Cook Time:** _____

## Ingredients

**Difficulty:** ☐ ☐ ☐ ☐ ☐

**Notes**

## Directions

Rating: ☆ ☆ ☆ ☆ ☆

Notes

| 57 | Name: |
|---|---|
| | Date: _____ Source: _____ |
| | ☐ Main Course  ☐ Baking  ☐ Starter  ☐ Dessert |

Servings: _____    Prep Time: _____    Cook Time: _____

## Ingredients

Difficulty: ☐ ☐ ☐ ☐ ☐

Notes

## Directions

Rating: ☆ ☆ ☆ ☆ ☆

Notes

58

Name: ........................................................................

Date: ..................... Source: ...........................................

☐ Main Course  ☐ Baking  ☐ Starter  ☐ Dessert

Servings: ............  Prep Time: ...............  Cook Time: ...............

## Ingredients

Difficulty: ☐ ☐ ☐ ☐ ☐

Notes

# Directions

Rating: ☆ ☆ ☆ ☆ ☆

Notes

Name: ........................................................................
Date: ........................  Source: ..................................................
- ☐ Main Course  ☐ Baking  ☐ Starter  ☐ Dessert

Servings: ..................  Prep Time: ..................  Cook Time: ..................

## Ingredients

Difficulty: ☐ ☐ ☐ ☐ ☐

Notes

## Directions

Rating: ☆ ☆ ☆ ☆ ☆

Notes

**Name:**

**Date:** _____  **Source:** _____

☐ Main Course  ☐ Baking  ☐ Starter  ☐ Dessert

**Servings:** _____  **Prep Time:** _____  **Cook Time:** _____

### Ingredients

Difficulty: ☐ ☐ ☐ ☐ ☐

**Notes**

# Directions

Rating: ☆ ☆ ☆ ☆ ☆

Notes

| | 61 | Name: |
|---|---|---|
| | | Date: _____ Source: _____ |

☐ Main Course ☐ Baking ☐ Starter ☐ Dessert

Servings: _____  Prep Time: _____  Cook Time: _____

## Ingredients

Difficulty: ☐ ☐ ☐ ☐ ☐

Notes

## Directions

Rating: ☆ ☆ ☆ ☆ ☆

Notes

| 62 | Name: ..................................................................... |
|---|---|
|  | Date: ........................ Source: ................................. |

☐ Main Course  ☐ Baking  ☐ Starter  ☐ Dessert

Servings: ................  Prep Time: ................  Cook Time: ................

## Ingredients

---

Difficulty: ☐ ☐ ☐ ☐ ☐

### Notes

## Directions

Rating: ☆ ☆ ☆ ☆ ☆

Notes

Name: ........................................................................................

Date: ....................  Source: ......................................................

☐ Main Course   ☐ Baking   ☐ Starter   ☐ Dessert

Servings: ..............  Prep Time: ..............  Cook Time: ..............

## Ingredients

------------------------------

------------------------------

------------------------------

------------------------------

------------------------------

------------------------------

------------------------------

------------------------------

------------------------------

------------------------------

Difficulty: ☐ ☐ ☐ ☐ ☐

Notes

## Directions

Rating: ☆ ☆ ☆ ☆ ☆

Notes

**Name:**

**Date:** _____  **Source:** _____

☐ Main Course  ☐ Baking  ☐ Starter  ☐ Dessert

**Servings:** _____  **Prep Time:** _____  **Cook Time:** _____

## Ingredients

**Difficulty:** ☐ ☐ ☐ ☐ ☐

Notes

## Directions

Rating: ☆ ☆ ☆ ☆ ☆

Notes

Printed in Poland
by Amazon Fulfillment
Poland Sp. z o.o., Wrocław
10 August 2022

0c5e93f7-365e-4743-8c76-653594fdf2ebR01